Daniel's Last Week

The Road to the Coming of the Lord

Daniel's Last Week

The Road to the Coming of the Lord

Elwood Trost

All scriptures are from the New King James Version unless otherwise

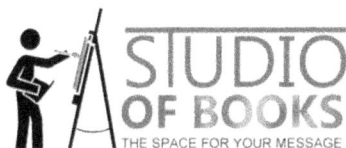

STUDIO OF BOOKS

THE SPACE FOR YOUR MESSAGE

Studio of Books LLC
5900 Balcones Drive Suite 100
Austin, Texas 78731
www.studioofbooks.org
Hotline: (254) 800-1183

Ordering Information:
Special discounts are available on quantity purchases by corporations, associations, and others. For details, contact the publisher at the address above.

Printed in the United States of America.

ISBN-13:	Softcover	978-1-970283-16-7
	eBook	978-1-970283-17-4
	Hardback	

Library of Congress Control Number:

Contents

Preface

After I received Jesus as my Lord and Savior and received the Holy Spirit. I received a hunger to read the bible and to study eschatology (the study of the end-times). Then, I discovered that one fourth of the bible is about the second coming of Christ.

My purpose for writing this book is to share some of the valuable insights that God has revealed to me.

Although it is important to know the end-time prophecies because we are living in the time when they are being fulfilled. It is not the most important thing because the most important thing we should be doing to prepare is working on our personal relationship with our Lord.

A relationship takes time and work, which means it takes more than just saying the sinner's prayer and being whisked off to heaven. The sinner's prayer is the starting point but not the finish line, and we are required to keep the faith to the end.

He who endures to the end shall be saved (Matthew 24:13).

Paul, in his second letter to Timothy, confirms this principle:

For I am already being poured out as a drink offering, and the time of my departure is at hand. I have fought the good fight, I have finished the race, I have kept the faith. Finally, there is laid up for me the crown of righteousness, which the Lord, the righteous Judge, will give to me on that Day, and not to me only but also to all who have loved His appearing (2 Timothy 4:6-8).

So, purpose in your heart today to never give up no matter how hard things might become and know God uses the hard times to mode us into His sons, and daughters.

This doesn't mean the study of end-time prophecy is not important and I suggest you should read it for yourself to give you the discernment to recognize the Antichrist. Deception was one the first signs Jesus warned us about and He said even the elect would be deceived if possible.

For false Christs and false prophets will rise and show great signs and wonders to deceive, if possible, even the elect. See, I have told you beforehand (Matthew 24-25).

The book of Revelation is the revelation of Jesus.

The Revelation of Jesus Christ, which God gave Him to show His servants—things which must shortly take place. And He sent and signified it by His angel to His servant John (Revelation 1:1).

The book by Daniel along with some types and shadows from the Old Testament give some keys to unlocking the book of Revelation.

The end-times prophecies are also evangelistic because when we see them fulfilled, we can say, "This is that." The bible is a book with history written in advance.

The end-time prophesies is one of the reasons I started reading the bible and seeking for some answers. What got my attention was I saw a presentation of about the signs of the second coming and Jesus was warning us about earthquakes. We had just experienced a 6.6 magnitude earthquake in San Fernando, California in1971. I became curious of who Jesus was that He could predict things 2,000 years in advance. The answer that I found was He could give us these signs, and we can know they will come to pass because He is God.

Therefore, let us seek a personal relationship with our Lord as a priority but at the same time let us be studying the end time prophecies that are being fulfilled and this time.

If you are reading this and didn't realize you could have a personal relationship with the Living God, please know you can, and this is how:

If you will admit you are a sinner and repent of your sins. And ask Jesus to come into your life. Jesus will forgive you and give you the Holy Spirit.

He was in the world, and the world was made through Him, and the world did not know Him. He came to His own, and His own did not receive Him. But as many as received Him, to them He gave the right to become children of God, to those who believe in His name: Who were born, not of blood, nor of the will of the flesh, nor of the will of man, but of God (John 1:10-13).

Father, give us the grace to endure and to keep the faith until the end. In Jesus name, Amen!

Introduction

There are many signs surrounding the second coming of Jesus, but there are two main signs from the book of Daniel that show us where we are on the road to the second coming. In chapter one, I will share what these two major signs are and how we can recognize them.

Knowledge is increasing and God is revealing more about the second coming of Jesus today and this is more of an incentive to get into God's Word. We should read the Bible ourselves and pray for the Holy Spirit to guide us. Knowing the word today is paramount in decerning deception and the lies of the enemy.

Paul, the apostle, warns us about a time that is coming when teachers will not stick to sound doctrine but will teach fables to tickle our ears:

I charge you therefore before God and the Lord Jesus Christ, who will judge the living and the dead at His appearing and His kingdom: Preach the word! Be ready in season and out of season. Convince, rebuke, exhort, with all long suffering and teaching. For the time will come when they will not endure sound doctrine, but according to their own desires, because they have itching ears, they will heap up for themselves teachers; and they will turn their ears away from the truth and be turned aside to fables. But you be watchful in all things, endure afflictions, do the work of an evangelist, fulfill your ministry (2 Timothy 4:1-5).

In chapter two, I will look at the signs Jesus gives us in Matthew chapter 24 and where they fit within our outline that Daniel gives us.

In Chapter three, we will look at the Seal Judgments of Revelation that expand and give us more information on the signs that Jesus gives us.

And in chapter four we will look at some types and shadows in the Old Testament and the New Testament that give us more insight into the second coming.

In chapter five, we will look at the description of God's mighty army.

By the time you get this book, we will probably be within Daniel's last week, which is referred to as Daniel's 70th Week. I am writing this book during the Feast of Trumpets, September 23-24, 2025. Many of us are seeing Daniel's 70th Week, the last seven years of this age, beginning during this feast.

Chapter One

The Road to the Second Coming

The book by Daniel gives us the outline of God's Road to the second coming.

In chapter nine of Daniel verses 24-27, we read about 70 weeks of years (490 years). 483 of the 490 years have been fulfilled with the crucifixion of Jesus; leaving one week (seven years) to be fulfilled just prior to the second coming of Jesus.

Let's look at verse 27:

> *And he will enter into a binding and irrevocable covenant with the many for one week (seven years), but in the middle of the week he will stop the sacrifice and grain offering [for the remaining three and one-half years]; and on the wing of abominations will come one who makes desolate, even until the complete destruction, one that is decreed, is poured out on the one who causes the horror (Daniel 9:27 Amplified Bible).*

When we see this covenant confirmed, we will know we are in the final seven years of this age. This is the beginning point of the road to the end of this age. When Jesus returns, He will set up His millennial reign which will bring peace to the earth for the next 1,000 years before it we go into eternity.

Then in the middle of this last week (3½ years), the Antichrist breaks this covenant and invades Israel and sits in the temple claiming to be God and demands to be worshipped. This begins the Great Tribulation that will last for 3½ years until the second coming of Jesus.

This covenant that will be confirmed and the "abomination of desolation," are the two main road signs that let us know where we are in relationship to our destination. If we miss the first sign, the second one will be obvious to us all.

What is interesting is that the U.N. is voting on such a covenant this September 2025 during the Feast of Trumpets. I will be looking forward to seeing if this could be the fulfillment of this covenant or not.

To recognize this covenant, it should give the Jews the right to begin their sacrifices, and the sacrifices should begin within six months. One of the things the Antichrist does at the midpoint is he breaks the covenant and invades Israel and stops the sacrifices.

When we see the "abomination of desolation," set up with the Antichrist sitting in the temple of God,it will be obvious to us all and then we will see Jesus coming through the clouds in 3½ years from that time. We might not know the day or hour, but we will know the season.

Chapter Two

Jesus' Gives us Signs

Jesus in chapter twenty-four of Matthew gives us signs to be watching for and He reveals to us where they fit within these last seven years. He does this by starting with the signs that fit within the first half of Daniel's 70th Week which He refers to as the "beginning of Sorrows" (Matthew 24:3-8)

These signs are to beware of deception; there will be wars and rumors of wars, famines, pestilences, and earthquakes. You might say this has been happening all along but what makes this different is that these are the final ones that we will never see again. These are the birth-pangs of the kingdom of God coming to earth.

It is interesting that Jesus referred to the "abomination of desolation," halfway through His discourse on the signs of the second coming in Matthew chapter 24. And the "abomination of desolation," happens halfway through the last seven years according to Daniel 9:27. I believe Jesus was giving us a clue of where the signs fit within Daniel's last week.

Then Jesus goes on to say that there would be great tribulation as the world has never seen (Matthew 24:16-28). From Scripture we know that the Antichrist gets to rule over the Middle East for these last 3½ years and that is why there will be great tribulation. This fits into the second half of our outline of the last week of Daniel.

And then in verse 29-31, Jesus describes His second coming and places it after the Great Tribulation.

To summarize; Jesus tells us what to expect the last seven years of this age. He begins with the "beginning of sorrows." which corresponds with the first 3½ years and then He mentions the "abomination of desolation, which falls in the middle the seven years, and then He puts the Great Tribulation in the last 3½ years. And then Jesus tells us His second coming is after it.

Now let's look at the Seals of Revelation to give us more revelation on the signs that Jesus gives us on the road to the second coming.

Chapter Three

The Seals of Revelation

The seals of Revelation expand and give us more insight into the signs that Jesus gave us.

Seal one:

> *Now I saw when the Lamb opened one of the seals; and I heard one of the four living creatures saying with a voice like thunder, "Come and see." And I looked, and behold, a white horse. He who sat on it had a bow; and a crown was given to him, and he went out conquering and to conquer (Revelation 6:1-2).*

The first thing Jesus warned us about was to beware of deception and the rider on a white horse is a picture of deception. The rider has a bow without arrows which indicates he is conquering by deception and without military force. The deception of the Antichrist will appeal to many because they don't know the Scriptures. He will deceive many by saying what they want to hear and how to solve the problems of the world, but God has other plans which is to bring His kingdom to earth.

Seal two:

> *"He opened the second seal, I heard the second living creature saying, "Come and see" Another horse, fiery red, went out. And it was granted to the one who sat on it to take peace from the earth, and that people should*

kill one another; and there was given to him a great sword (Revelation 6:3-4).

Jesus tells us there will be wars and rumors of wars. The seven years began with a peace treaty and now war has broken out over the earth. This rider is given a great sword which could indicate the use of nuclear weapons.

Seal three:

When He opened the third seal, I heard the third living creature say, "Come and see." So, I looked, and behold, a black horse, and he who sat on it had a pair of scales in his hand. And I heard a voice in the midst of the four living creatures saying, "A quart of wheat for a denarius, and three quarts of barley for a denarius; and do not harm the oil and the wine" (Revelation 6:5-6).

The third seal gives us more details on what Jesus said about famines. This seal reveals that inflation will increase until it takes a day's wages to buy a loaf of bread.

Seal four:

When He opened the fourth seal, I heard the voice of the fourth living creature saying, "Come and see." So, I looked, and behold, a pale (green) horse. And the name of him who sat on it was Death, and Hades followed with him. And power was given to them over a fourth of the earth, to kill with sword, with hunger, with death, and by the beasts of the earth (Revelation 6:7-8).

With the opening of the fourth seal, we are now halfway through Daniel's 70th Week. It is interesting that there are no more riders, and this is because we are now at the middle of the last seven years, and the Antichrist rules the next 42 months. This is when the Great Tribulation begins which will last for 3½ years until Jesus returns and defeats the Antichrist.

The good news is that it appears that the Antichrist only rules over one fourth of the earth, which is the countries that surround Israel, but he will have influence over the whole world.

It is time to get your name written in Lamb's Book of Life, if you haven't done that yet. It is going to take patience and faith to get through this time and a personal relationship with the Lord.

When the world seems to be falling apart, The Antichrist will seem to have the answers that people want to hear and many will be deceived and take the "mark of the beast," giving their allegiance to him and sealing their doom.

This supports the concept that the seals are being opened chronologically at one-year intervals, which means seals 1-3 will fulfill the first three years. Seal four will fulfill the fourth year with 3½ years falling in the middle of it when the Antichrist comes into power. Then seals 5,6, and 7 will be fulfilled in the last 3 years.

Seal five:

When He opened the fifth seal, I saw under the altar the souls of those who had been slain for the word of God and for the testimony which they held. And they cried with a loud voice, saying, "How long, O Lord, holy and true, until You judge and avenge our blood on those who dwell on the earth?" Then a white robe was given to each of them; and it was said to them that they should rest a little while longer, until both the number of their fellow servants and their brethren, who would be killed as they were, was completed (Revelation 6:9-11).

Persecution is coming to all nations to test our faith. When the "mark of the beast," is given out and we cannot buy of sell for the next 3½ years, it will take faith to resist taking it.

There is Scripture that explains how the people of God are protected during the Great Tribulation. It is found in Revelation chapter 12 where we read about the woman who is Israel today that consists of all who believe in their Jewish Messiah have a place in the wilderness prepared by God to protect them and feed them for 1260 days, time, times, and half a time, the 3½ years of the Great Tribulation. It is her offspring that has been sealed to go through this time and war with the Antichrist.

Seal Six:

I looked when He opened the sixth seal, and behold, there was a great earthquake; and the sun became black as sackcloth of hair, and the moon became like blood. And the stars of heaven fell to the earth, as a fig tree drops its late figs when it is shaken by a mighty wind. Then the sky receded as a scroll when it is rolled up, and every mountain and island was moved out of its place. And the kings of the earth, the great men, the rich men, the commanders, the mighty men, every slave and every free man, hid themselves in the caves and in the rocks of the mountains, and said to the mountains and rocks, "Fall on us and hide us from the face of Him who sits on the throne and from the wrath of the Lamb! For the great day of His wrath has come, and who is able to stand?" (Revelation 6:12-17).

The seals are adding information to the signs Jesus gave us.

In Matthew when Jesus describes His second coming and the resurrection/rapture (Matthew 24:29-31). He mentions the cosmic signs of the sun and the moon in the same verses, and they appear to be happening at the same time as He returns, but if one seal is opened each year, this reveals that there could be a space of a year or more between these cosmic signs and the actual second coming.

This is important to know because the sixth seal is not the second coming but a warning that the wrath of God is coming this last year and is completed by Jesus after He returns and the "last trump." This means that it is only the last year of the seven tribulation that is the wrath of God and not all seven years like many believe.

The question is asked, "Who is able to stand?" This question is answered in next chapter when 144,000 are sealed to go through it. Then chapter seven concludes with a harvest of souls that are too great to be counted.

One reason God allows the Great Tribulation is to bring people to repentance so they can be saved. The Great Tribulation is God's harvest time, and Jesus told us that the laborers are few and to pray that God would send laborers into the harvest. If God asked you to be part of this harvest, what would your answer be?

Seal seven:

When He opened the seventh seal, there was silence in heaven for about half an hour. And I saw the seven angels who stand before God, and to them were given seven trumpets. Then another angel, having a golden censer, came and stood at the altar. He was given much incense that he should offer it with the prayers of all the saints upon the golden altar which was before the throne. And the smoke of the incense, with the prayers of the saints, ascended before God from the angel's hand. Then the angel took the censor, filled it with fire from the altar, and threw it to the earth. And there were noises, thundering's, lightnings, and an earthquake. So, the seven angels who had the seven trumpets prepared themselves to sound (Revelation 8:1-6).

When the seventh seal is opened the last year, the wrath of God begins and it is tempered to bring more into the kingdom, but they will be those who will continue to harden their hearts and resist salvation. The next chapters of the book of Revelation describe the trumpet judgments and at the seventh trumpet, "last trump," Jesus returns and resurrects/raptures His elect (1 Corinthians 15:51-52; Revelation 11:15).

And then the bowl judgments are poured out after the second coming to complete the wrath to God and those who have taken the "mark of the beast," will have to endure them.

Chapter Four

Types and Shadows

God has given us types and shadows that reveal more information on how the end-times unfold. One type and shadow of the second coming is the Exodus account.

Pharoah being a type of the Antichrist and Moses and Aaron being a type of the two prophets of Revelation chapter 11. The Israelites being protected from the judgments of God being a type of the woman of Revelation chapter 12 being protected during the last 3½ years. The crossing of the Red Sea being a type of resurrection/rapture. And Jesus being the greater Moses leads a military campaign up through Jordon into the promise land. (Isaiah 63:1-6; Malachi 3:1-16). However, this campaign will only take ten days this time and not 40 years.

The feasts of the Lord which are prophetic also. There are seven feasts (Leviticus 23). The spring feasts were fulfilled to the day and hour by Jesus at His first coming. They are Passover, Feast of Unleavened Bread, Feast of First Fruits. Jesus was crucified on Passover, buried on Unleavened Bread, raised from the dead on the Feast of First Fruits.

Fifty days later, the Feast of Weeks or Pentecost was fulfilled when the Holy Spirit was poured out on the church.

The fall feasts are to be fulfilled at the second coming. They are the Feast of Trumpets, the Day of Atonement, and Feast of Tabernacles.

Jesus returns on the Feast of Trumpets and leads a military campaign up through Jordan on His way to Jerusalem which takes ten days. We get our ten days because the Feast of Trumpets takes place on Tishri one and the Day of Atonement on Tishri ten.

The kings of the East know Jesus is marching to Jerusalem and surround it believing they can defeat Him. When Jesus' foot touches the Mount of Olives, Armageddon takes place on the Day of Atonement, and it is all over.

Five days later, "the marriage supper of the Lamb" begins on the Feast of Tabernacles on Tishri fifteen. It will take place on earth with real food and real wine.

Another type and shadow that confirms one seal being opened each year of Daniel's 70th Week is God's instructions to Joshua for the battle of Jericho (Joshua 6:1-6).

They marched around Jericho one time a day for six days. If we have one day equals a year, we see something interesting. The first six seals being opened one year apart for the first six years. On the seventh day they were to march around Jericho seven times, blowing their trumpets. This represents the opening of the seventh seal beginning the seventh year and The Trumpet Judgments of Revelation sounding the last year of the seven years.

At the last trumpet, they were to shout. Jesus comes back with a shout of an arch angel and trumpet sounding. This is a type of the second coming at the end of Daniel's 70th Week.

Jericho walls falling is symbolic of the fall of the Antichrist and Rahab being protected and brought out is a type of the elect being protected resurrected/raptured at the end of the Great Tribulation.

Then God's army marched up and burned Jericho is a type of the bowl judgments and Jesus' military campaign that completes God's wrath.

Another type and shadow are the three Hebrew children that wouldn't bow down to the statue that Nebuchadnezzar had set up. They were thrown into a furnace heated seven times hotter than normal. The fire was so hot that those who threw them into the fire perished. Nebuchadnezzar asked, "Who is the fourth man in this furnace because we only threw in three." The fourth man was Jesus. This is a type and shadow of the elect of God being in the fire of the Great Tribulation and Jesus being with us and protecting us.

Also, many see the six days of creation as a timeline of when the last seven years begin. The six days of creation representing 6,000 years of human history, and the one day of rest representing the 1,000-year millennial reign of Christ.

This would put the return of Jesus 2,000 years after the crucifixion which took place in year 4,000. This gives us a window of the second coming between 2030 to 2033.

Let's see what happens on this Feast of Trumpets this year, September 23-24, 2025. If Daniel's 70th begins then, the "abomination of desolation," would happen on Passover in 2029, and the second coming will be on the Feast of Trumpets in 2032. It is interesting in Israel the Feast of Trumpets is referred to as the feast that no one knows the day or hour.

It is also interesting that this year they did something in Israel as far as I know has never been done. On the Feast of Trumpets 2025, they had at one time and they broadcasted it to the whole world.

This idea one day equals one thousand years is also applied to a verse from Hosea:

Come and let us return to the Lord; For He has torn, but He will heal us; He has stricken, but He will bind us up. After two days He will revive us; On the third day He will raise us up, that we may live in His sight (Hosea 6:1-2).

Israel was restored in 1948 which would be within the two days or 2,000 years that they would be revived, and the third day would be the millennial reign of Jesus when they will live in His sight.

Noah's flood is a type and shadow of the wrath of God. God didn't take Noah to heaven and then bring him back after the flood. He protected Noah through the flood.

It is interesting from the time the foundations of the deep were opened and rain started to the time they were able to set foot on land again was one year and ten days. This is the same amount of time that I have for the wrath of God beginning with the trumpet judgments which last one year and Jesus military campaign lasting ten days.

And it came to pass after seven days that the waters of the flood were on the earth. In the six hundredth year of Noah's life, in the second month, the seventeenth day of the month, on that day all the fountains of the great deep were broken up, and the windows of heaven were opened. And the rain was on the earth forty days and forty nights (Genesis 7:10-12).

And:

And it came to pass in the six hundred and first year, in the first month, the first day of the month, that the waters were dried up from the earth; and Noah removed the covering of the ark and looked, and indeed the surface of the ground was dry. And in the second month, on the twenty-seventh day of the month, the earth was dried. Then God spoke to Noah, saying, 'Go out of the ark (Genesis 8:13-16).

I have said this once, but it is worth repeating. There is Scripture that explains how the people of God are protected during the Great Tribulation. It is found in Revelation chapter 12 where the woman who is Israel today that consists of all who believe in their Jewish Messiah have a place in the wilderness prepared by God to feed her and protect her for 1260 days, time, times, and half a time, the 3½ years of the Great Tribulation. It is her offspring that has been sealed to go through this time and war with the Antichrist.

Another type and shadow is when a king returns from war, his subjects would go out to meet him and usher him back into their city.

The next day a great multitude that had come to the feast, when they heard that Jesus was coming to Jerusalem, took branches of palm trees and went out to meet Him, and cried out: "Hosanna!" "Blessed is He who comes in the name of the Lord! The King of Israel!" (John 12:12-13).

When Jesus returns, we will be caught up to meet Him in the air and usher Him back to the earth to help Him set up His millennial reign.

Chapter Five

God's Mighty Army

God's army consists of the resurrected followers of Jesus. Jesus came the first time as the "Lamb of God," but He is coming the second time as the "Lion of the Tribe of Judah."

Some might think God destroying the wicked is extreme and not like their God of love, but we must remember God has had great patience and given everyone time to repent and those who will be experiencing God's wrath are those who would not repent and have given their allegiance to Satan, i.e, the Antichrist, They have rejected salvation giving God no other choice Because God has given everyone freewill to choose who they would serve.

God's army is described in the following Scriptures:

Let the high praises of God be in their mouth, and a two-edged sword in their hand, to execute vengeance on the nations, and punishments on the peoples; To bind their kings with chains, and their nobles with fetters of iron; To execute on them the written judgment—This honor have all His saints. Praise the Lord! (Psalm 149:6-9).

Another description of God's army is found in the book of Joel:

Blow the trumpet in Zion and sound an alarm in My holy mountain! Let all the inhabitants of the land tremble; For the day of the Lord is coming, for it is at hand: A day of darkness and gloominess, A Day of clouds and thick darkness, Like the morning clouds spread over the mountains. A People come, great and strong, the like of whom has never been; Nor will there ever be any such after them, even for many successive generations. A fire devours before them, and behind them a flame burns; The land is like the Garden of Eden before them, and behind them a desolate wilderness; Surely nothing shall escape them. Their appearance is like the appearance of horses; And like swift steeds, so they run. With a noise like chariots Over mountaintops they leap, Like the noise of a flaming fire that devours the stubble, like a strong people set in battle array. Before them the people writhe in pain; All faces are drained of color. They run like mighty men, they climb the wall like men of war; Everyone marches in formation, and they do not break ranks. They do not push one another; Everyone marches in his own column. Though they lunge between the weapons, they are not cut down. They run to and fro in the city, they run on the wall; They climb into the houses, they enter at the windows like a thief. The earthquakes before them, the heavens tremble; The sun and moon grow dark, And the stars diminish their brightness. The Lord gives voice before His army, For His camp is very great; For strong is the One who executes His word. For the day of the Lord is great and very terrible; Who can endure it? (Joel 2:1-11).

This army is made up of resurrected saints, and this is why they are invincible, so if you haven't found your ministry yet, don't give up because you might be being prepared to be part of this mighty army.

I see something interesting in the army that destroys Jericho that makes it a type and shadow of this army that is described in Joel:

Now Jericho was securely shut up because of the children of Israel; none went out, and none came in. And the Lord said to Joshua: "See! I have given Jericho into your hand, its king, and the mighty men of valor. You shall march around the city, all you men of war; you shall go all around the city once. This you shall do six days. And seven priests shall bear seven trumpets of rams' horns before the ark. But the seventh day you shall march around the city seven times, and the priests shall blow the trumpets. It shall come to pass, when they make a long blast with the ram's horn, and when you hear the sound of the trumpet, that all the people shall shout with a great shout; then the wall of the city will fall down flat. And the people shall go up every man straight before him (Joshua 6:1-6).

Notice, the people shall go up every man straight before him and the description of what it says about this army in Joel:

They run like mighty men, they climb the wall like men of war; Everyone marches in formation, and they do not break ranks. They do not push one another; Everyone marches in his own column. Though they lunge between the weapons, they are not cut down (Joel 2:7-8).

So, the people shouted when the priests blew the trumpets. And it happened when the people heard the sound of the trumpet, and the people shouted with a great shout, that the wall fell down flat. Then the people went up into the city, every man straight before him, and they took the city. And they utterly destroyed all that was in the city, both man and woman, young and old, ox and sheep and donkey, with the edge of the sword (Joshua 6:20-21).

I believe this is more confirmation that the battle of Jericho is a picture of the second coming of Jesus and His mighty army destroying the Antichrist.

Moses also saw this mighty army:

Now this is the blessing with which Moses the man of God blessed the children of Israel before his death. And he said: "The Lord came from Sinai and dawned on them from Seir; He shone forth from Mount Paran, And He came with ten thousands of saints; From His right hand came a fiery law for them. Yes, He loves the people; All His saints are in Your hand; They sit down at Your feet; Everyone receives Your words" (Deuteronomy 33:1-3).

One of the best descriptions that I have found in the Bible that describes Jesus' military campaign at His second coming is recorded in Habakkuk chapter 3:

A prayer of Habakkuk the prophet, on Shigionoth. O Lord, I have heard Your speech and was afraid; O Lord, revive Your work in the midst of the years! In the midst of the years make it known; In wrath remember mercy. God came from Teman, The Holy One from Mount Paran. His glory covered the heavens, And the earth was full of His praise. His brightness was like the light; He had rays flashing from His hand, and there His power was hidden. Before Him went pestilence, and fever followed at His feet. He stood and measured the earth; He looked and startled the nations. And the everlasting mountains were scattered, the perpetual hills bowed. His ways are everlasting. I saw the tents of Cushan in affliction; The curtains of the land of Midian trembled. O Lord, were You displeased with the rivers, Was Your anger against the rivers, Was Your wrath against the sea, That You rode on Your horses, Your chariots of salvation? Your bow was made quite ready; Oaths were sworn over Your arrows. You divided the earth with rivers. The mountains saw You and trembled; The overflowing of the water passed by. The deep uttered its voice and lifted its hands on high. The sun and moon stood still in their habitation; At the light of Your arrows they went, At the shining of Your glittering spear. You marched through the land in indignation; You trampled the nations in anger. You went forth for the salvation of Your people, For salvation with Your Anointed. You struck the head from the house of the wicked, by laying bare from foundation to neck. You thrust through with his own arrows The head of his villages. They came out like a whirlwind to scatter me; Their rejoicing was like feasting on the poor in secret. You walked through the sea with Your horses, Through the heap of great waters. When I heard, my body trembled; My lips quivered at the voice; Rottenness entered my bones; And I trembled in myself, That I might rest in the day of trouble. When he comes up to the people, He will invade them with his troops (Habakkuk 3:1-16).

This portion of Scripture is more understandable if we realize that mountains are symbolic for governments, and the sea is symbolic of the people, and horses are symbolic of power.

Habakkuk completes this chapter and his book with a song of praise:

Though the fig tree may not blossom, Nor fruit be on the vines; Though the labor of the olive may fail, And the fields yield no food; Though the flock may be cut off from the fold, And there be no herd in the stalls—Yet I will rejoice in the Lord, I will joy in the God of my salvation. The Lord God is my strength; He will make my feet like deer's feet, And He will make me walk on my high hills (Habakkuk 3:17-18).

This is a good attitude for us to have as we enter the coming days.

Conclusion

The main purpose of this book is to eliminate some of the confusion about the second coming and reveal to us when to expect the return of Jesus. It will happen 3½ years after we see the "abomination of desolation."

Jesus mentions the "abomination of desolation," halfway through his discourse in Matthew chapter 24. And Daniel 9:27 places it in the middle of Daniel's 70th Week.

Therefore, this is the major sign that we should be watching for, and Paul tells us that we will not be gathered to the Lord before we see the "abomination of desolation," in his second letter to the Thessalonians:

Now, brethren, concerning the coming of our Lord Jesus Christ and our gathering together to Him, we ask you, not to be soon shaken in mind or troubled, either by spirit or by word or by letter, as if from us, as though the day of Christ had come. Let no one deceive you by any means; for that Day will not come unless the falling away comes first, and the man of sin is revealed, the son of perdition, who opposes and exalts himself above all that is called God or that is worshiped, so that he sits as God in the temple of God, showing himself that he is God (2 Thessalonians 2:1-4).

Our hope should be in the resurrection, and not a rapture that precedes it.

I have shared what the Lord has revealed to me about His second coming and I hope it helps you understand the end times and what is unfolding today.

The second coming is closer than many believe, and now is the time to prepare and not to wait until we are in the Great Tribulation. We can prepare physically for a difficult time but the main way to prepare is by pressing into a closer relationship with our Lord.

All this information is useless unless it brings an urgency for us to change areas of our heart that are not in alignment with God's heart.

We should be asking ourselves, does my comfort and the things of this world mean more to me than my relationship with God? If so, God is giving us time to repent. So, let's not delay. This is a time to get right with God because soon we will be standing before Him and giving an account of our time here on earth.

It is appointed for man to die once and after this the judgment (Hebrews 9:27).

Our God is merciful and kind, but He is also righteous and holy. It is time for us to start living for God and get out of our comfort zone of living for self:

But the fruit of the Spirit is love, joy, peace, longsuffering, kindness, goodness, faithfulness, gentleness, self-control. Against such there is no law. And those who are Christ's have crucified the flesh with its passions and desires. If we live in the Spirit, let us also walk in the Spirit. Let us not become conceited, provoking one another, envying one another (Galatians 5:22-26).

Those who are Christ have crucified the flesh with its passions and desires. And we know crucifixion is not fun or pleasant, but it is necessary to separate the wheat from the chaff.

Enter by the narrow gate; for wide is the gate and broad is the way that leads to destruction, and there are many who go in by it. Because narrow is the gate and difficult is the way which leads to life, and there are few who find it (Matthew 7:13-14).

Let's conclude with this prayer that King David gave us:

Search me, O God, and know my heart; Try me and know my anxieties; And see if there is any wicked way in me and lead me in the way everlasting (Psalm 139:23-24).

Let us pray for this and mean it with all our heart. In Jesus' name. Amen!

Thanks for watching with me

www.ingramcontent.com/pod-product-compliance
Lightning Source LLC
Chambersburg PA
CBHW052125030426
42335CB00025B/3115